# THE BIG CLICK:

*Photographing Wisconsin*

*Memorial Day Weekend*
*May 24-27, 1991*

9:00 p.m., Friday *Memorial Day weekend brings thousands of Illinois residents to Wisconsin. Many have summer homes here and others drive north just to play. The welcome mat is out in a way highway travelers understand as demonstrated by this handsome sign along major artery I-94.*

Shawn J. O'Malley

# THE BIG CLICK:

*Photographing Wisconsin*

*Memorial Day Weekend, 1991*

SPONSORS

Banc One Wisconsin
  Corporation
Hardee's
Rayovac Corporation
ShopKo Stores, Inc.
Midwest Express
  Airlines
Eastman Kodak Co.,
  Consumer Imaging
  Division
Qualex, Kodalux
  Processing Services
San Francisco Hilton
  on the Square
The Dallas Parkway
  Hilton
The New York Hilton
  and Towers
Chicago Hilton and
  Towers
Harry W. Schwartz
  Bookshops
The Camera Company,
  Madison
WISN-TV, Milwaukee
WLUK-TV, Green Bay
WSAW-TV, Wausau
WEAU-TV, Eau Claire
  and La Crosse
WMTV, Madison

6:30 p.m., Sunday
*A spectacular wide-angle perspective atop Rib Mountain Tower reveals the part of the Wisconsin River Valley known as the Wausau Area. "A faraway place," as its Indian name declares, Wausau and Marathon Counties are known for such diversity as milk, cheese, paper, food processors, Case industrial cranes, Fiskars knives and scissors and giant Wausau Insurance Companies.*

Chip Henderson

11:00 a.m., Monday
*Mary Hanneman turned shutterbug at the annual Memorial Day parade in Monona, south of Madison. She enhanced her appropriate dress with a couple of flags in her hair. "I am very thankful to have my brothers Danny and Chuck back from the Persian Gulf. I thought my own outfit was very patriotic."*

Jon Lee

Library of Congress Catalogue Number 91-92850
Hardcover ISBN # 0-942399-14-5

Printed in The United States of America

Produced by Lightworks and Broadcast Concepts Inc., Cary, North Carolina, in cooperation with Wisconsin television stations and sponsors.

Lightworks, 6005 Chapel Hill Road, Raleigh, North Carolina 27607 (919) 851-0518

Broadcast Concepts Inc., 1135 Kildaire Farm Road, Suite 200-31, Cary, North Carolina 27511 (919) 460-7596.

*Wisconsin map: American Automobile Association, 1990*

4:30 p.m., May 22, Interstate 94. The sky looked bad, with mocking clouds and frequent streaks of lightning coming every few seconds. Cindy Byrum and I were heading west from Milwaukee to Madison where a group of *Big Click* sponsors and photographers were gathering at the Governor's Mansion. The car radio was turned off so we did not know how truly unpromising the weather reports were — tornado watches and the general miserable, muggy weather that is more typical of spring in other parts of the country.

The occasion in Madison was the kickoff of a statewide four-day event called *The Big Click: Photographing Wisconsin*. Scheduled for Friday and the weekend surrounding Memorial Day, it was expected to have more professional and amateur photographers taking more pictures than at any time in the state's history. Many months of preparation were coming together this very week. One thing you look for at a time like this is good weather. And it was raining.

As we reached Cambridge Road in Madison, preparations were in their final stages. Everything was in order. Tommy Thompson has a back yard on beautiful Lake Monona with a view of the State Capitol to the northwest. He had just returned from Washington, but was gracious and relaxed, as were all of the television station staff, the various *Big Click* sponsors, the mayors and state legislators, and photographers.

The sun broke through just before Elmer Childress' live

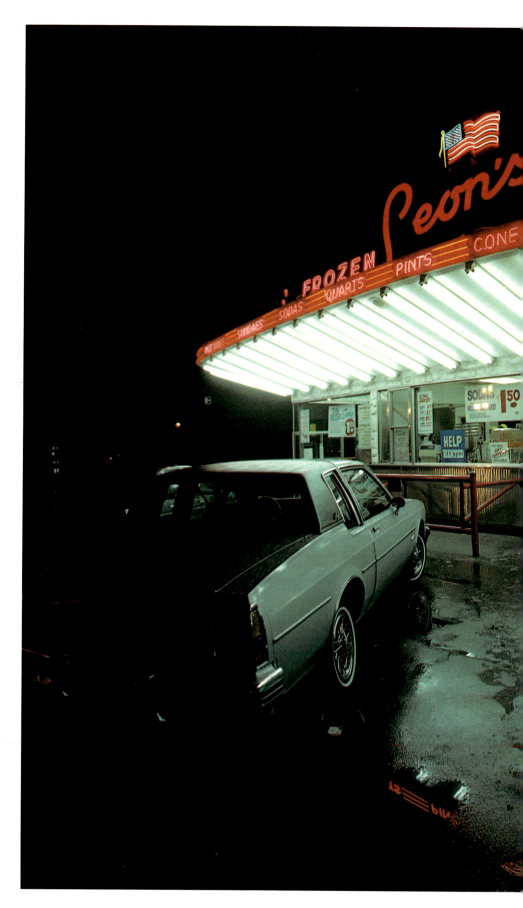

11:30 p.m., Saturday
*Leon's Custard on
South 27th Street in
Milwaukee is modeled
after Big Al's of
"Happy Days."
Although no longer
featuring drive-up
service with wait-
resses on roller skates,
it still offers a real
'50s atmosphere and
good custard.*

Scott Morris

9

8:45 p.m., Sunday
*College students shared the sunset at Rib Mountain Park, Wausau.*

Chip Henderson

weather spot was seen by WMTV's south-central area audience and followed by a couple of very pleasant hours of friendly talk, food, mansion-touring and delightful harp music.

These rain showers were not the only ones during that week in May, but the timely clearing on that late afternoon in Madison seemed to be providential for the bulk of the four days of *The Big Click*. And, as we saw later, the variety of weather, from thick fog to billowy cumulus clouds, provided wonderful shades and hues not possible with constant "ideal" weather.

From the thousands of images taken on May 24-27 and submitted for consideration at least one idea comes through. It is the people and places that are important to Wisconsinites that they want to portray, that they want to share with any of us who will take the time. We'll take the time.

— *Jane Collins*

1:00 p.m., Monday
*Finally a clear night in Milwaukee afforded an impressive skyline complete with full moon over Lake Michigan at Veteran's Park.*

Scott Morris

11:50 p.m., Friday
*Leslie Ziolek plans a*
*corner pocket shot at*
*Earl's Bar in Kenosha*
*as part of her start to*
*the holiday weekend.*

Shawn J. O'Malley

7:42 p.m., Sunday
*Greyhounds run average speeds of 40-45 mph at Dairyland Greyhound Park, the world's largest dog track. Dairyland opened June, 1990, providing more than 800 jobs in the Kenosha area.*

Shawn J. O'Malley

8:17 p.m., Sunday
*Dogs and handlers are accustomed to big crowds. The park is open year round and is set between Chicago and Milwaukee, making it accessible to approximately 12 million people.*

Shawn J. O'Malley

4:00 p.m., Friday
*Van der Geest
livestock outside of
Wausau.*

Chip Henderson

3:00 p.m., Friday
*Edward Roeder, 84, relaxes in the yard of his Wausau dairy farm. The farm, his family's for more than 100 years, will pass to his daughter-in-law. Mr. Roeder farmed until 1975, then leased out the land. The tree which shades him today was brought from Tigerton by his father when Edward was a young boy.*

Chip Henderson

9:15 a.m., Saturday
*A tugboat is vital for the 2.6 million tons of cargo going in and out of the Port of Milwaukee each year.*

T. J. Florian

10:52 a.m., Saturday
*On a cold, very foggy morning at least one tug is visible at work pulling the* Ikan Selayang *freighter into port. The Singapore vessel will deliver steel coils on this trip.*

T. J. Florian

3:00 p.m., Monday
*Fredrick Redi-Mix in Waukesha has all of its red, white and blue trucks lined up while workers take a long weekend. Prior to 1970, the trucks were painted various colors. Then Richard Fredrick Sr.'s son Dale graduated from West Point Military Academy and the new color scheme was adopted.*

T. J. Florian

7:15 a.m., Friday

*Places like this one, where men come to chat and exchange stories, do exist. "We call this the liars' bench," shouted Leonard Erickson, who has frequented the bench outside Anderson's Store in Coon Valley for many years. He and his friends meet almost every morning. Said Henzil Hanson, "The personnel has changed so much through the years. I've been coming here every morning for about twenty years, except in the winter. My lungs can't take it then." Seated from left to right are Bennet Koll, Henzil Hanson, Hjalmer Stenslien and Leonard Erickson.*

Jon Lee

10:15 a.m., Monday
*School House Beach,*
*Washington Island.*

Mike Brisson

6:30 a.m., Sunday
*Sand Bay, Door
County.*

Mike Brisson

10:00 a.m., Monday
*Leland Haase, Berun,
carries flag as part of
color guard at
Memorial Day
services in Omro,
west of Oshkosh. A
former Marine, he has
been a VFW member
since 1946.*

James R. Koepnick

11:00 a.m., Saturday
*4th U.S. Army Band
in Bayview parade.*

Bruce Krueger

11:15 a.m., Friday
*In the cemetery at Wisconsin Veterans Home in King, a couple places flowers at a relative's grave.*

Mike Brisson

HARVEY W HEIDEMAN
PFC
US ARMY
WORLD WAR II
APR 18 1906
MAY 6 1975

3:30 p.m., Sunday
*Mud racing at Iron
County ATV Rally
in Hurley.*

Darryl R. Beers

11:30 a.m., Monday
*Whitewater kayaker
on Wolf River,
Langlade County.*

Darryl R. Beers

9:30 a.m., Friday
*Heather Florian
attends Mrs. Mary
Kowalski's kindergar-
ten class at Meadow-
brook School in
Pewaukee.*

T. J. Florian

10:30 a.m., Sunday
*Crowd pleasers at*
*Vilas Park Zoo are*
*polar bears Nanuq*
*and Aurora. Nanuq*
*was brought to*
*Madison's zoo on*
*Lake Wingra in 1988.*
*Aurora, Nanuq's*
*female companion,*
*was born in 1982,*
*and came on loan*
*from Milwaukee in*
*1989.*

Mary Langenfeld

5:45 p.m., Friday
*Brad (in pink
trunks) and Brian
Auxier relax in their
pool after a hard day
at school.*

Bonnie Auxier

4:10 p.m., Saturday
*Judy Lombard, who does garden design and maintenance, is purchasing plants for a church in town at Always Blooming Nursery, Wausau. Her business, Settlement Greenhouse and Garden Design, was named for a lawsuit that supported her and led her into her own business.*

Chip Henderson

9:00 a.m., Friday
*Mathilda "Tilly"
Matz was born 101
years ago on Memo-
rial Day. She was also
married in 1918 on
Memorial Day. "So
we'd have one very
special day." She was
actually born on a
boat coming from
Russia, just as it came
into the port of New
York. Her family
settled in Coleman,
WI; she later moved to
Wausau, then to
Milwaukee. A
garment worker by
trade, she still enjoys
sewing; she just needs
someone to thread the
needle for her. At
Alexian Village, a
retirement and skilled
care facility in
Milwaukee where she
now lives, someone
will thread her
needles.*

Jane Gleeson

8:00 p.m., Saturday
*It was far from an ideal night for a carnival, but in Menomonee Falls the Knights of Columbus Memorial Weekend event went on as planned.*

Henry H. Smith

9:00 a.m., Friday
*A brief period of proper instruction can lead to many years of swimming pleasure and safety, as shown at Pewaukee Beach.*

David L. Denemark

6:50 p.m., Monday
*Couples are often found venturing onto the rocks of Milwaukee's shoreline, but this trip was special for Gregory Jamerson and Vicki Underwood. The two had met just an hour earlier. Jamerson's line, "Guess who's coming to dinner?" caught Underwood's attention as she snacked with friends and the two struck up a conversation.*

Gary Dineen

4:55 a.m., Friday
*Jansen's Restaurant, Waupaca.*

Mike Brisson

5:20 p.m., Friday
*Trucks off Highway 54 West, Waupaca; drivers inside at Jansen's.*

Mike Brisson

7:05 p.m., Sunday
*The Trempealeau River winds from northern Trempealeau County and meets the Mississippi River here in Perrot State Park, north of La Crosse. It flows into a bay at the foot of Trempealeau Mountain. Once open water, the bay has filled in and now is mostly marsh, as is happening all along the Mississippi tributaries. Not good for fish, but great for birds.*

Richard L. Staszewski

6:52 p.m., Sunday
*Tranquil farm scene near Aztalan State Park in southern Wisconsin's Jefferson County.*

T. J. Florian

3:00 p.m., Monday
*U.S. Coast Guard
Great Lakes Station,
Milwaukee.*

Peter Draves

5:00 a.m., Saturday
*Foggy morning at
Port of Kewaunee.*

Mike Brisson

2:18 p.m., Sunday
*A cow strikes a pose similar to the sign at Junction D near Cashton.*

Jon Lee

9:00 a.m., Friday
*Ernest Haugen on his
small farm in Coon
Valley. The Jerseys
are gentle. Ernest and
his brother Joseph
inherited the land
from their parents.
"We are free to do
what we like," said
Ernest. Of the cows,
he said, "It sure helps
when they are tame."*

Jon Lee

45

9:15 a.m., Sunday
*Commercial fishing is the way of life for this Door County family who settled in the area in the 1800s. From left, Emery Weborg, Howard Weborg, Wallace Weborg and Tim Weborg (Wallace and Tim are father and son) carry on the long tradition on the bay of Green Bay and Lake Michigan.*

Mike Brisson

11:00 a.m., Sunday
*Jessie Lee, 6, (left) and brother Robin, 7, fish for trout at Larson's Bridge, Coon Valley. This is the same spot that their father Jim fished when he was their age.*

Jon Lee

47

2:00 p.m., Saturday
*Luke Auxier visits
Uncle Al at Neenah
Fire Station #2. Luke
announces, "I hope
you know, I'm a
fireman now."*

Bonnie Auxier

3:15 p.m., Friday
*Oshkosh and the Fox
River.*

Dr. Leroy L. Zacher

1:30 p.m., Monday
*Youngsters observed
from South Shore
Park, Milwaukee.*

T. J. Florian

51

8:30 p.m, Sunday
*The Van Douser
Tower at Rib Moun-
tain State Park
affords a restful view
of dairy farms in late
day.*

Chip Henderson

8:00 a.m., Sunday
*Jeff and Joe Loomis at*
*St. Croix River near*
*Louise Park.*

Fred Loomis

10:15 a.m., Saturday
*Yerkes Observatory,
one of the first
important observato-
ries in the country, is
sponsored by the
University of Chicago
and is built on a hill
overlooking William's
Bay and Lake Geneva.*

Darryl Jordan

9:30 a.m., Friday
*Nicholas Gajewski reads a story about a farm to his class at Meadowbrook School kindergarten, Pewaukee.*

T. J. Florian

9:15 a.m., Friday
*Mrs. Mary Kowalski
prepares her kinder-
garteners for their
upcoming field trip to
a farm.*

T. J. Florian

10:20 a.m., Friday
*Singing games are
enjoyed by Mrs.
Kowalski's class.*

T. J. Florian

12:05 p.m., Sunday
*Allison Herzog on carousel at Circus World Museum, Baraboo. It was a choice between Circus World and the lake that Allison's mother made at the last moment.*

Craig Robinson

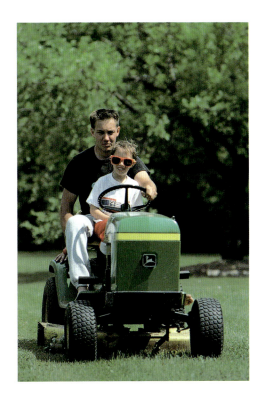

2:00 p.m., Sunday
*Russell Zimmermann gets a little help from his son Joshua as he uses his riding lawnmower to mow his front lawn near Sheboygan Falls.*

Sam Arendt

6:00 p.m., Sunday
*Two-year-old Jordan Vinson plays on his tractor in Stoddard.*

Jon Lee

1:30 p.m., Saturday
*Close quarters for the train engineer at Milwaukee County Zoo.*

Thomas Moran

3:20 p.m., Monday
*A view of South Shore
Marina and the
Milwaukee skyline.*

Peter Draves

9:50 a.m., Sunday
*Procession into All
Saints Cathedral
before mass. The
cathedral is known
for its Anglo-Catholic
rituals, and for its
social ministry for
those who are men-
tally ill.*

Bruce W. Buchanan

9:00 a.m., Sunday
*Reverend Robert Stub, past dean of All Saints Cathedral, Milwaukee.*

Bruce W. Buchanan

10:00 p.m., Friday
*Congratulations are in order after Waukesha South High School beat Muskego High School, 9-1.*

Timothy P. Snopek

2:00 p.m., Saturday
*Nichole Larson dons her feather at Menominee Veterans Pow-wow in Keshena. A dancer for 14 years, she was recently featured in a Wisconsin travel commercial.*

Chip Henderson

2:20 p.m., Saturday
*Jeff Woerpel, 25,
Escanaba, MI,
member of Bay de Noc
tribe from Upper
Michigan at Menom-
inee Veterans Pow-
wow in Keshena.
Woerpel has been
dancing for 16 years
because, "It's fun; I've
got friends all over the
circuit. I travel all
summer long." His
clothing "evolved,
starting with red and
adding more neon
colors in the last
couple of years."*

Meg Jones

3:00 p.m., Sunday
*Ned Peller,*
*Milwaukee, rock*
*climbing at Devil's*
*Lake.*

James R. Koepnick

11:00 a.m., Monday
*Gushing waters and unique rust-colored rock formations attract tourists to Dave's Falls County Park near Amberg.*

Lila Aryan

5:18 p.m., Sunday
*Mill Bluff State Park, southeast of Tomah, features 100-foot sandstone bluffs.*

Craig Robinson

1:00 p.m., Sunday
*Birches' Lodge on Boot Lake, Springstead.*

Shelly Anne Cavins

11:00 a.m., Saturday
*Stephen Landolt (in*
*Santa suit) and Staff*
*Sgt. (SSG) John L.*
*Babl of the 1157th*
*Army National*
*Guard Unit of*
*Oshkosh and Berlin*
*on parade route from*
*Omro to Oshkosh.*

Minimay Smith

2:45 p.m., Saturday
*Fans cheer at Milwaukee County Stadium as Brewers rally to tie Cleveland and then go ahead 4-3 by scoring 4 runs in the 8th inning. Brewers eventually lose 5-4 in the 9th inning.*

Gary Dineen

10:15 p.m., Sunday
*Bartollata fireworks
display at Milwaukee
County Stadium.*

Peter Draves

8:30 p.m., Saturday
*The familiar spin of colored lights on the midway were especially welcomed on the foggy evening of the Knights of Columbus Memorial Weekend in Menominee Falls.*

Henry H. Smith

6:15 p.m. Sunday
*Wendy Petrie, Rt. 1
in Stoddard, leads
her horse along a
country creek. "It's
peaceful walking
around with our
horses; a chance to
get away. You're free
to run or walk. There
are no boundaries,"
said Wendy.*

Jon Lee

12:15 p.m., Saturday
*Mrs. Don Hah of Combined Locks playing bingo. She and five or six other women share the winnings of their four or five hours of play daily. During the summer the Girls Fun Bank Account grows until it is split or used together at season's end. So far this year there is $1,700 in the account.*

Chip Henderson

12:30 p.m., Saturday
*Menominee Indian Reservation Bingo Parlor.*

Chip Henderson

2:20 p.m., Monday
*It was sunny and registering in the 80s as Milwaukee met the Detroit Tigers at County Stadium. The Brewers eventually lost 15-9 in 14 innings.*

Gary Dineen

1:00 p.m., Monday
*Milwaukee Brewers
on standby.*

Gary Dineen

3:00 p.m., Monday
*The east shore's Port Washington.*

Debra J. Bartlein

12:15 p.m., Sunday
*David Sparacino snaps Elizabeth Kenny and Abe Lincoln. But will he turn in this photo to The Big Click? The three are in front of Federalist-style Bascom Hall at the University of Wisconsin-Madison.*

Mary Langenfeld

80

6:45 a.m., Sunday
*Theresa M. LaCrax has worked for nine months at this Wausau Hardee's. She works a 45-hour week because she needs the money.*

Chip Henderson

4:30 p.m., Monday
*Except for the newer model cars, you might think you've been transported back to the '50s and '60s when you eat at Ardy & Ed's Drive-In in Oshkosh. Car hops hustle to take your order on roller skates; music of 30 and 35 years ago plays over the loudspeaker. Marie Canziani, a junior at Oshkosh Lourdes High School, is spending her second summer working at the Drive-In, maintaining her roller skating skills and saving money for college.*

Mary Jones

6:35 p.m., Sunday
*Cherie Vinson of
Stoddard plays with
her goat, Periwinkle,
in the doorway of an
old shed. Says Cherie,
"She's not fun to ride
but she is to pet. She
eats dog and horse
food. I think she
thinks she's a dog or a
horse."*

Jon Lee

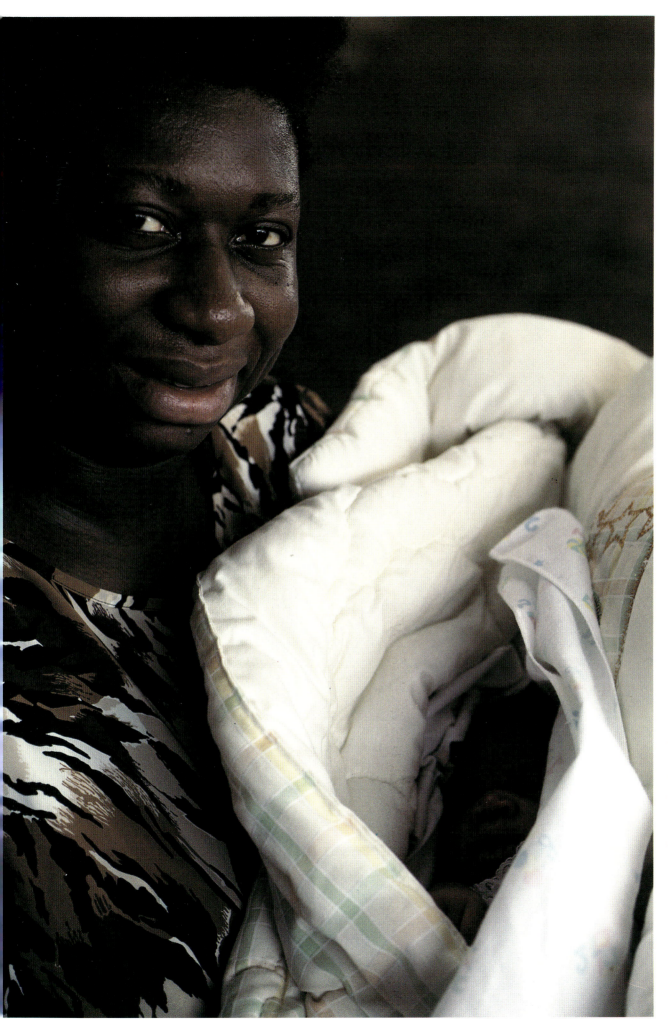

2:00 p.m., Friday
*Mrs. Angela Jenkins
with day-old daughter
Melissa as they leave
Sinai Samaritan
Hospital in Milwau-
kee.*

Jane Gleeson

3:00 p.m., Saturday
*MK3 Tony Ferrill,*
*engineer, BM1 Linda*
*Wedge (inside),*
*coxswain, and*
*Seaman Randal Croat*
*make up this U. S.*
*Coast Guard Station*
*crew in Milwaukee.*

Barbara L. Jakopac

12:40 p.m., Sunday
*Ken Larsen of
Palatine, IL, at Gills
Rock on the bay of
Green Bay.*

Mike Brisson

4:00 p.m., Monday
*Wood carver Hank Scholten assembles a spinning wheel that he is currently working on in his shop in Franklin in rural Plymouth. He also makes life-size wooden Indians and wildlife carvings.*

Sam Arendt

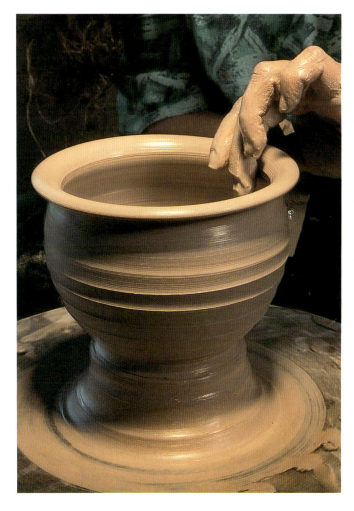

2 :00 p.m., Sunday
*This piece at Idlewild Pottery, just south of Sturgeon Bay, is the work of Wendy Woldt, owner. She specializes in white slip and glazing techniques often using her own glaze recipes.*

Scott Neuville

10:30 a.m., Sunday
*Flyfishing is a joy for Clarence Moilien of Coon Valley. Said Clarence as he fished in Spring Coulee, "I feel relaxed. I'm away from everything and with nature."*

Jon Lee

5:30 p.m., Monday
*Boats must pass
through locks on the
Mississippi River at
Alma.*

Chip Henderson

6:30 p.m., Sunday
*Aerial view of Fontana, Lake Geneva.*

Darryl Jordan

9:32 a.m., Saturday
*Cases of Milwaukee
beer destined for
Russia are being
loaded at the port of
Milwaukee.*

T. J. Florian

2:15 p.m., Monday
*Bradford Beach,
Milwaukee.*

Robert L. Smith

6:30 p.m., Monday
*Henry Rickerman
takes a break from the
spring heat at the
house in Waukesha
where he has lived
since 1956.*

Timothy P. Snopek

2:30 p.m., Sunday
*At North Country Taxidermy, Hazelhurst, Marvin Smith works on one of the 150 birds he'll mount this year. Marvin has been at this work for more than 30 years and annually stuffs 250 deer, 500 fish and about 30 bears. Advertising is by word of mouth.*

Chip Henderson

7:50 p.m., Monday
*Looking south over the Mississippi River valley from Grandad's Bluff in La Crosse.*

Richard L. Staszewski

2:30 p.m., Sunday
*The steam driven
Kettle Moraine
locomotive between
North Lake and
Merton.*

Barbara L. Jakopac

6:00 p.m., Sunday
*The railway is run by volunteers who enjoy trains like Steven Butler and Mike Michaud.*

Barbara L. Jakopac

4:30 p.m., Saturday
*Al Johnson, owner of Al Johnson's Swedish Restaurant of Sister Bay, is surrounded by part of his staff of 30 waitresses. Johnson began the business 43 years ago as a coffee shop; in time he expanded the restaurant, added a boutique and a furniture store. The popular Door County restaurant is recognizable for its grass roof where goats graze freely.*

Mike Brisson

5:00 p.m., Friday
*Branko Radicevic sits
in one of the best
Serbian restaurants
anywhere, his own.
Three Brothers in
Milwaukee is a family-
run restaurant for
three generations.
Branko and his wife
Patricia do the cooking.
"A recent customer
said, 'So many memo-
ries of my youth — so
many memories of my
grandmother's home.' I
don't think there could
be a better compliment
than when someone
connects good feeling of
the family with my
restaurant. What could
be better?"*

Bruce W. Buchanan

11:00 a.m., Monday
*Eric Martin, 12, of*
*Walworth shoots a*
*basketball.*

Darryl Jordan

**3:15 p.m., Monday**
*A wonderful expansive view of Washington County is the reward of those who climb the 178 steps to the top of the steeple of Holy Hill Church, Hubertus.*

Todd Ponath

11:00 a.m., Monday
*Sydney Hih Building
at Third Street and
Juneau, Milwaukee.*

T. J. Florian

107

6:45 p.m., Sunday
*Farmlands of the rich
Wausau region.*

Chip Henderson

6:00 a.m., Friday
*Mother and calf on a
Waupaca farm.*

Mike Brisson

10:15 a.m., Saturday
*Part of welcoming home ceremonies and responses for the 1157th Army National Guard Unit of Oshkosh and Berlin from Operation Desert Storm duty.*

Minimay Smith

12:30 p.m., Saturday
*Spc. Brian Johnson
and wife Michelle of
Berlin exchange close-
up greeting at the
National Guard
Armory in Oshkosh
after the official
release from duty in
Operation Desert
Storm. The couple
was married just prior
to Johnson's deploy-
ment to the Persian
Gulf.*

Minimay Smith

12:00 noon, Monday
*Ken Cady, Omro,*
*drives his jet boat*
*along the Fox River*
*near Eureka.*

James R. Koepnick

1:00 p.m., Monday
*Third Street Pier
Yacht Club.*

T. J. Florian

8:45 a.m., Monday
*There aren't enough hours in the day for Vince Bugner. During the week he works full time delivering mail; nights and weekends are spent on the farm and here his lambs are fully occupied with mealtime.*

Shawn J. O'Malley

10:32 a.m., Saturday
*Under the edge of the Blue Mounds, the highest point in southern Wisconsin, Andrew Cosby Johnson leads a tour of the cave of the mounds. At a constant 50 degrees F. the caves are a cool, damp place of geological beauty, and Andrew shows the highlights to the members of the tour. Andrew is 17 and a junior at Verona Area High School.*

Craig Robinson

8:00 p.m., Friday
*A studio shot planned for* The Big Click *turned out fine from the outsider's point of view at Mark Gubin's in Milwaukee.*

Mark Gubin

6:15 p.m., Friday
*Five hundred or so Milwaukee Yacht Club members and guests enjoyed a social hour before the annual "commissioning" ceremony which officially opens the boating season.*

Jane Gleeson

7:00 p.m., Friday
*At the Milwaukee Yacht Club ceremony, Coast Guardsmen receive last minute instructions from Wayne Zuehls, right. From left, they are Andy Jepson, Tom Olson, Tom Sheehy, Steve Hoss and Zuehls.*

Jane Gleeson

*8:30 a.m., Friday*
*Dr. Terence M. Schmahl and his top cardiac surgical team replace the mitral heart valve of their patient. The chest cavity is packed with ice to lower body temperature and the patient is maintained on a heart-lung machine. Dr. Schmahl, who was instrumental in the implant of the Jarvik-7 artificial heart in 1986, is performing this surgery at St. Luke's Medical Center in Milwaukee. St. Luke's has become a leading center for coronary medicine.*

Peter Draves

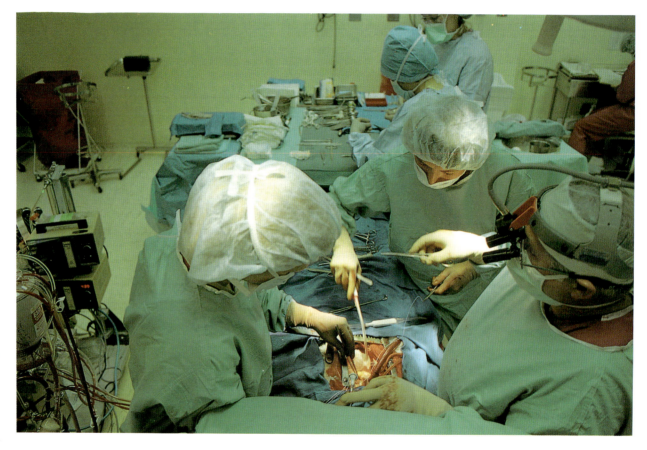

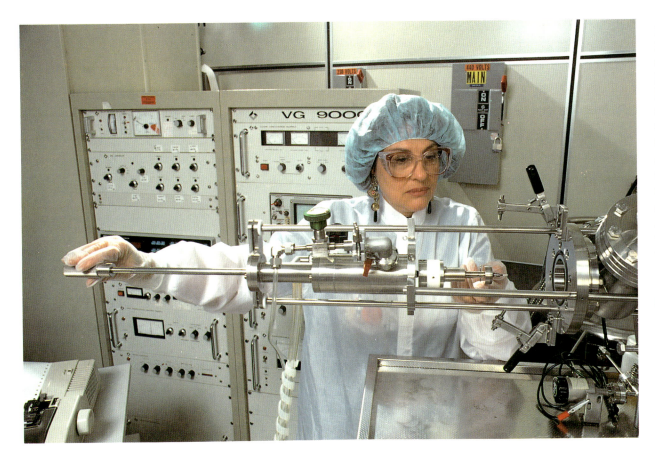

10:10 a.m., Friday
*Technology of tomorrow is the business of General Electric Medical Systems, the Waukesha-based division of General Electric. Marlene Adland works with a high-tech instrument called a Glow Discharge Mass Spectrometer which is used in research to analyze unknown substances.*

Robert J. Alberte, Jr.

9:15 a.m., Sunday
*In the repair shop at the Mid-Continent Railway Museum in North Freedom, Art Oseland is fixing the springs on the center plate of the frame of a steam locomotive by freeing it of dust and rock.*

Craig Robinson

7:52 p.m., Monday
*A train chugs through the La Crosse Country Club.*

Richard L. Staszewski

9:45 a.m., Sunday
*One of 400 volunteers
at the Mid-Continent
Railway Museum in
North Freedom.*

Craig Robinson

1:30 p.m., Monday
*Diane Raeder of Glenbeulah in dress appropriate for the setting, is cording wool in the summer kitchen of the Wade House Historical Complex in Greenbush. Built in 1850 to serve the traffic on the busy Sheboygan and Fond du Lac Plank Road, the Wade House Inn was the culmination of the efforts of Sylvanus and Betsey Wade, enterprising Yankee settlers, and their family to build a center of civilization here in the Wisconsin wilderness.*

Ralph E. Adamson

2:30 p.m., Sunday
*Rafting on Menom-*
*inee River. One*
*adventurer from*
*Milwaukee, Bonnie*
*Gundrum said, "I*
*liked screaming just*
*as we dropped into*
*'Volkswagen Rock' —*
*fantastic ride!"*

Thomas J. Parker

7:45 p.m., Monday
*Niagara Paper Mill in northern Marinette County at dusk.*

Thomas J. Parker

10:00 a.m., Monday
*Patriotic Caddy in the
Omro Memorial Day
Parade.*

James L. Koepnick

12:45 p.m., Sunday
*Billy Carter rests outside a store along Old Highway 51 he has rented for the last two months to stash and sell his goods. "Buying the stuff is easy, but selling it sometimes isn't." He gets his stuff from friends and old farmhouses.*

Chip Henderson

5:40 p.m., Sunday
*Conner Lake in*
*Flambeau River*
*State Forest.*

Nancy Pass

7:15 p.m., Sunday
*Wind surfer near*
*High Cliff State Park,*
*Lake Winnebago.*

Dr. Leroy L. Zacher

7:45 p.m., Friday
*Stock car races at Luxemburg speedway are a Friday night tradition.*

Mike Brisson

8:20 p.m., Friday
*The headdress is right.*

Mike Brisson

5:50 a.m., Monday
*First light on the
eastern shore of
Washington Island,
Lake Michigan.*

Mike Brisson

9:00 a.m., Friday
*Don Hansen delivers vets who need assistance to various locations at the Wisconsin Veterans Home in King. The headlight on his driving cart is useful in the underground tunnels which he travels by using a "tugger system."*

Mike Brisson

12:45 p.m., Saturday
*Kirk Knight adjusts the tie of Eric Hawkins outside Sacred Heart Catholic Church, Oshkosh. The groomsmen are part of the Paul Witt and Karen Hawkins wedding which will be underway at 1:00 o'clock.*

Mary Jones

12:17 p.m., Sunday
*Everybody likes the
balloons, especially
the giraffe who likes
purple balloons best.
The Circus World
Museum in Baraboo
has been called " . . .
the most exciting,
noisy and color-
splashed museum you
will ever see" by the
Boston Globe.*

Craig Robinson

10:05 p.m., Sunday
Tyler Jentz makes
cheese fudge and
must mix it with his
bare hands at the Bob
& Sherry Schuh
Family Farm in
Freedom. Observing
is Pat Horth of New
London, looking
conspicuous in cow
costume.

Bonnie Auxier

6:30 p.m., Monday
*Off Highway 88
between Cream and
Gilmanton.*

Chip Henderson

8:32 a.m., Friday
*Juliana Akstulewick,*
*78, of Menasha writes*
*letters to his relatives*
*from the Wisconsin*
*Veterans Home in*
*King.*

Mike Brisson

The following signs appear within the image:

NO SMOKING
IN TUNNEL

PUT OUT ALL
SMOKING
MATERIALS

| → | Marden Center |
| ← | Burns Clemens |
| ← | Central Services |
| ← | Stordock Hall |
| ← | Olson Hall |

8:55 a.m., Friday
*Sweeping up at the
Wisconsin Veterans
Home.*

Mike Brisson

10:00 a.m., Saturday
*Barbara Foster is library director in Hancock, Waushara County. This small, 90-year old building does not provide enough space for their books and a new location is planned. Hancock's population is 419.*

James R. Koepnick

7:12 a.m., Friday
*An early morning bus ride starts another school day for third-grader Timmy Patrick of Pleasant Prairie. Timmy's mom and dog, Brandy, come to see him off.*

Shawn J. O'Malley

**7:52 p.m., Monday**
*From the top of
Grandad's Bluff, this
late May day reveals
La Crosse as lush
green, dotted with
light buildings and
other bits of color, and
featuring the arched
span of the Main
Channel Bridge.*

Richard L.
    Staszewski

1:17 p.m., Monday
*Milwaukee skyline.*

T. J. Florian

7:45 p.m., Monday
*Sunset on Fox River
between Lake
Winnebago and
Butte des Morts.*

Mark Picard

7:00 p.m., Monday
*Farm along Highway
10 near Eleva.*

Chip Henderson

10:45 a.m., Sunday
*"On the way to
various locations in
Brookfield I was
drawn to Wisconsin
Memorial Park. It is
beautiful and peaceful
there, but it also holds
a special, personal
significance for me."*

Jennifer Frankovis

12:30 p.m., Sunday
*Isaac Lathrop admires his cat, Junior, from a rustic-looking window on a Stoddard farm. "If I get another cat, I'll call her 'Midnight,'" said Isaac.*

Jon Lee

154

10:00 a.m., Saturday
*Another black cat poses from a safe position in south Sheboygan County, east of Silver Creek.*

Sam Arendt

155

7:00 a.m., Saturday
*At Lady of Visitation Chapel, Sister Coronita is participating in the mass as she does each morning. She is 87 years old, born in Milwaukee. She taught school for 50 years. When the photographer thanked her for her gracious spirit and for allowing the photos to be taken of her, she replied, "I'm going to put you on my special prayer list. I'll just tell Jesus who you are and He'll drop your name in the chalice."*

Mary Catanese-Pugens

9:58 a.m., Sunday
*Mass is about to begin at All Saints Cathedral, Milwaukee.*

Bruce W. Buchanan

157

6:15 p.m., Monday
*Jodi Forseth and
Jessica Griffiths feed
a thirsty calf.*

Jan Day

6:00 p.m., Monday
*Brian Rohloff milks
cows on the Rohloff
family farm near
Whitewater.*

Rick Miller

159

12:00 noon, Monday
*Wayne Hart of*
*American Legion Post*
*#544, Twin Lakes,*
*stands at attention in*
*Memorial Day*
*tribute.*

Christine A.
Verstraete-Prucha

1:00 p.m., Sunday
*"They're all so very special." At Woods National Cemetery.*

Caspar de Jongh

7:10 p.m., Sunday
*Rainbow southwest
of Kohlsville.*

Tim Stoffel

6:00 p.m., Sunday
*Aerial of farm north
of Elkhorn.*

Darryl Jordan

6:30 p.m., Monday
*Courtney McKenna
in an undisturbed
moment at a picnic in
her backyard.*

Susan Townsend

3:00 p.m., Monday
*Brian Arnold may be
thinking, "That's it
for the work. I will
sit right here 'til the
party starts."*

Darla Lange

3:00 p.m., Monday
*Amanda Burk gets to know chicks on farm located on County Trunk A near Janesville.*

Rick Miller

9:00 p.m., Friday
*Blomsness All-Star Carinval rides light the parking lot in Racine.*

James Enright

9:05 p.m., Friday
*The ride attendant
explains, "Every year
we come and build
overnight; lasts two
maybe three nights,
then tear down and
move on!"*

James Enright

8:00 p.m., Monday
*Silos on a quieted
Wisconsin dairy
farm, just off Abbott
Road in south
Sheboygan County.*

Sam Arendt

3:15 p.m., Sunday
*Dale Kunkle and his daughter, Sue, of Rosendale happily paint a fire hydrant in patriotic colors. Rosendale doesn't have a city water system so the hydrant is actually sort of a ruse. It marks one of several cisterns located in the city which store water for the volunteer fire department; Dale is a volunteer fireman.*

Mary Jones

6:30 p.m., Monday
*From Buena Vista Park, the Mississippi River winds past the Dairyland Power Cooperative. A coal-burning plant, the Alma station generates 184,090 kw of electric power.*

Chip Henderson

2:15 p.m., Friday
*Gordy Foust, left, and
Randy Walotka
secure HEMTT
wrecker (U.S. Army's
Heavy Expanded
Mobility Tactical
Truck) on railroad
flat beds en route to
Las Alamitos, CA.
These vehicles were
used in Operation
Desert Storm for
towing disabled
vehicles. Oshkosh
Truck Corporation is
said to be the free
world's largest
producer of heavy-
duty military trucks.*

Dr. Leroy L. Zacher

7:00 a.m., Saturday
*The black and white of several boats blend into the gray of early morning on Sturgeon Bay.*

Mike Brisson

10:42 a.m., Monday
*Jim Trummel and*
*'Lady' have been*
*riding in parades for*
*about eight years.*
*They are in about 40*
*parades each year. We*
*caught up with them*
*on this beautiful,*
*sunny day in West*
*Allis.*

Bruce Krueger

8:00 a.m., Sunday
*Jim Rieder established Timber Wolf Farm in 1967 in an effort to protect the endangered Eastern Timber Wolf and restore it safely to the wilds. Here Jim breaks from cleaning enclosures and feeding wolves to show affection to Nantan, a six-year-old female wolf.*

Marny A. Malin

5:00 p.m., Friday
*It is unlikely that David Okhahah will find his photograph here. He is homeless, but takes odd jobs in his neighborhood near Walker Street in Milwaukee to make his way. "I have pride, but it is not always easy to keep it," he says.*

Sarah McEneany

6:30 a.m., Sunday
*Susan Dunn and her
dog Emily walk along
Waters End Road in
Door County.*

Mike Brisson

10:30 p.m., Saturday
*Bradford Beach,*
*Milwaukee.*

Greg Nelson

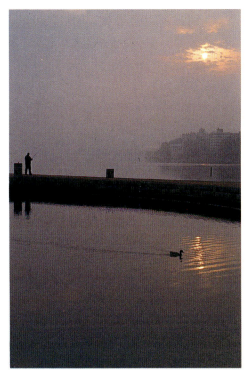

6:00 a.m., Friday
*Fishing near University of Wisconsin-Madison campus.*

Paul McMahon

8:00 a.m., Sunday
*Farmer's wares on*
*back of his truck,*
*Cedarburg.*

Raymond Eurich

6:45 a.m., Sunday
*Robert Johansen of Racine sketches a scene of Sand Harbor at Sand Bay in Door County while sitting on the commercial fishing boat named "Hope."*

Mike Brisson

183

3:30 p.m., Monday
*A 25-foot, 10-inch link chain made from a 21-foot white pine log is just one of the fascinating carvings at Carl's Wood Art Museum in Eagle River. Ken Schels, son of Carl who started Schels Lumber Company in 1949, carved the chain using a chainsaw. He says that separating the links is the delicate part; each weighs 30 pounds. Ken has no formal art training, but his favorite works have buyers. The coach of the Chicago Bears, Mike Ditka, purchased one of Ken's chain saw-carved bears and has ordered six more.*

Mark Picard

4:00 p.m., Monday
*Brewers vs. Detroit.*
*Say bleacher fans:*
*"It's mine!"*

Gary Dineen

4:30 p.m., Monday
#4 *Paul Molitor in*
*action against Tigers.*

Gary Dineen

11:45 a.m., Monday
*Pre-game ceremonies*
*on Memorial Day*
*included a military*
*fly-by following the*
*National Anthem and*
*throwing of the first*
*pitch by U. S. war*
*veterans.*

Gary Dineen

1:15 p.m., Saturday
*In the 4th inning of the Milwaukee Brewers vs. Cleveland Indians game, Jim Gantner fields and throws for the third out.*

Gary Dineen

1:00 p.m., Sunday
*Heidi Stobbe of
Berlin makes a last
check before leaving
home for graduation
exercises.*

John Iwatta

11:30 a.m., Sunday
*Jerome J. Maksaytis,*
*Father "Max" stands*
*before the Berlin*
*High graduating*
*class in the sanctuary*
*of St. Stanislaus*
*Catholic Church as*
*he prepares to deliver*
*his baccalaureate*
*address.*

John Iwatta

11:15 a.m., Monday
*Bob Masnado and*
*daughter Sarah, 1, at*
*Monona's Memorial*
*Day parade: "Sarah*
*was waving two flags*
*at one point — she*
*really got excited*
*when the clowns*
*came by," said her*
*dad.*

Jon Lee

4:00 p.m., Sunday
*Chantell Ako, 5,*
*would agree with*
People Magazine's
*high rating of Babcock*
*ice cream, which is*
*produced by the*
*University of Wiscon-*
*sin-Madison dairy*
*science department.*
*Chantell and her*
*family came to*
*Madison from the*
*Ivory Coast so that*
*her father could*
*pursue a master's*
*degree in civil*
*engineering here.*

Mary Langenfeld

10:00 a.m., Friday
*Ernest Haugen and his brother Joseph work a small farm in Coon Valley. Ernest has piled quite a stock of fence posts, 148 to be exact. "I can make about 10 per hour, and I usually make some over 100 each year," says Ernest. The Haugens make good use of their timber land. Remarked Ernest, "Using wood fence posts (as opposed to steel) keeps our expenses down. We have been making them for 46 years." The brothers also prefer to not use chemicals.*

Jon Lee

10:45 a.m., Saturday
*Russ Kirchmeyer of Phillips and his woodpile. "Here's how I feel after all the work's done!" he smiles.*

Nancy Pass

3:30 p.m., Monday
*Kacie cools off. Dad
snaps the fun.*

Jerry Seil

7:05 p.m., Saturday
*After the rain, shoes and clothing dry by a fire at Durward's Glen near Baraboo. A group has been photographing in the rain all afternoon.*

Mourad Arganian

7:15 a.m., Monday
*Early morning
canoeing, Marshall
Park, Middleton.*

Kevin M. Roth

6:00 p.m., Sunday
*Racine Harbor.*

Joshua Smith

8:30 p.m., Sunday
*Sunset over Fox
River, Voyageur
Park, DePere.*

Lori A. Wisnicky

5:30 a.m., Monday
*Fishermen at dawn at
52nd Street pier on
Lake Michigan,
Kenosha.*

Michael Arbet

8:45 p.m., Friday
*Milwaukee's skyline
at dusk from South
Shore Yacht Club.*

Greg Nelson

3:30 p.m., Saturday
*Canoeists on the*
*Sheboygan River*
*near Kiwanis Park.*
*Cold temperatures,*
*light mist, and the*
*resultant fog on the*
*river is the setting for*
*this sequence.*

Duane W. Hopp

8:00 a.m., Friday
*A misty scene begins
the weekend in
McKinley Park.*

Jennifer Frankovis

11:45 a.m., Monday
*A great sound came out of the east and the photographer turned his camera upward. The jet fly-in over Milwaukee County Stadium coincided with the playing of the national anthem.*

Timothy G. Abler

10:30 a.m., Friday
*These colorful hands*
*are the artwork of*
*kindergarteners at*
*Meadowbrook School.*

T.J. Florian

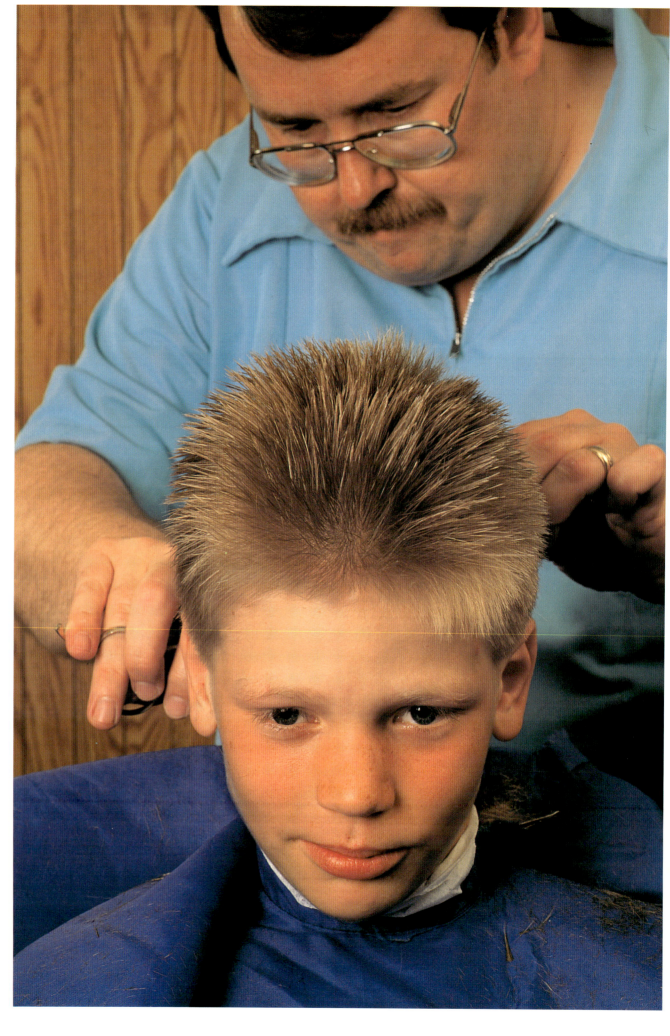

5:30 p.m., Friday
*Adam Evans,*
*Merrill, at the*
*trained hands of*
*barber Mike*
*Chrudimski.*

Chip Henderson

2:15 p.m., Friday
*John Kapal has been a barber in the same location on Milwaukee's south side for 61 years. His shop is more than a place to get a haircut. John is one of the last remaining members of the Sandlot Baseball team who played in Milwaukee in the '20s. He's in the Sandlot Baseball Hall of Fame. The basic haircut takes John 20 minutes. "Here's where you can get a good cut."*

Barbara L. Jakopac

9:30 p.m., Saturday
*Celebration 101 at*
*Voyager Park, De*
*Pere.*

Patrick Ferron

5:30 p.m., Monday
*Matt Hofmann at J.J.'s Drive-In, Eagle.*

Mary Osmundsen

4:30 p.m., Monday
*Maryann B. Fojtih
and her accordian
provided something of
a reunion for Big
Click photographer
Nancy Pass. Mary-
ann, of Phillips, gave
Nancy accordian
lessons for five years
in nearby Catawba
when Nancy was a
child.*

Erol Reyal

208

2:30 p.m., Sunday
*Menominee Indian
Powwow, Keshena.*

Pauline G. Collins

11:15 a.m., Monday
*Dan Schwandt, 14, at*
*Memorial Day*
*Parade, Riverside*
*Memorial Cemetery,*
*Appleton. Dan is a*
*member of the Third*
*Wisconsin Veteran*
*Volunteer Infantry, a*
*Civil War re-enact-*
*ment group. His*
*father, Donald*
*Schwandt is also a*
*member.*

Guy Peterson

11:30 a.m., Monday
*Four sisters, all Fox River Area Girl Scouts, are also in the parade in Appleton. They are twins Kathleen and Theresa, 9, Sadie, 10, and Tracy, 7.*

Guy Peterson

211

12:15 p.m., Saturday
*The city of Oshkosh is eager to welcome the 1157th Transportation Group of the Army National Guard, returning home after duty in Operation Desert Storm.*

Mary Jones

10:25 a.m., Monday
*A pre-church service on Washington Island on Memorial Day honored Boy Scouts, Girl Scouts and Veterans.*

Mike Brisson

8:00 p.m., Friday
*Wequiock Falls,*
*Green Bay.*

Mike Brisson

2:00 p.m., Friday
*Lawrence Kare,*
*Mequon, a cash crop*
*farmer.*

Sarah McEneany

2:30 p.m., Saturday
*Buffalo belonging to*
*Myrtle and Marvin*
*Feldman at their*
*ranch on Highway 57*
*look like brown woolly*
*lumps rising from the*
*earth, further muted*
*in tone by the hazy*
*skies.*

Jane Gleeson

8:00 a.m., Sunday
*Coon Valley,*
*Lutheran Church*
*and farm owned by*
*Robert Lee.*

Jon Lee

1:15 p.m., Monday
*Near Maxville, urea
fertilizer is put on
rows of young potato
plants. More than 400
acres have been
planted with Russell-
Burbank potatoes.*

Chip Henderson

6:00 p.m., Monday
*Small business person
Michelle Tittl of
Plymouth did very
well with a lemonade
stand that she opened
at 4:30 in the after-
noon. At 10 cents a
glass, she attracted
the entire neighbor-
hood.*

Sam Arendt

11:35 a.m., Monday
*The bright midday sun illuminates the red, white and blue garb of this familiar landmark, the Pabst Brewing company of Milwaukee.*

T. J. Florian

12:30 p.m., Friday
*For Nancy Pass this scene is a familiar one: a child, Lexi Knowles, curiously examines these uncommon sculptures. They are at Fred Smith's Concrete Park on Highway 13, a few miles south of Phillips. Fred Smith, now deceased, was an inspired artist who started making monumental cement sculptures with bottles and glass collected from his tavern next door. His work depicted scenes of folk lore and personal visions. The residents dismissed him as looney until he gained some notoriety when a European public television crew came to film the park. His work has shown in some prestigious museums.*

Erol Reyal

3:00 p.m., Monday
*"Our two boys, Eric and Kevin, cooling off with popsicles."*

Nancy Back

11:00 a.m., Monday
*Ryan Bachorz at Riverside Park, Neenah.*

Joyce Nottleson Moon

5:11 p.m., Sunday
*Alesha Buskager, 2, photographer's granddaughter, at Camp Awana Missionary Conference.*

Joyce KenKnight

8:30 p.m., Monday
*Countryside west of Blue Mounds State Park.*

Scott Ausenhus

6:30 p.m., Friday
*Wisconsin Avenue,*
*Milwaukee.*

Mark Gubin

5:35 a.m., Saturday
*South Shore lakefront,
Milwaukee.*

Harold Saichek

2:00 p.m., Friday
*Mindy Triebold
nurses son Adam in
their Whitewater
home.*

Rick Miller

10:00 a.m., Monday
*Allison Wojt,*
*Waterbury Inn,*
*Ephraim.*

Rose Gulcynski

6:00 p.m., Monday
*Jennifer and Andrea*
*Snavely going home*
*to Plover from*
*Mequon.*

Cheryl Snavely

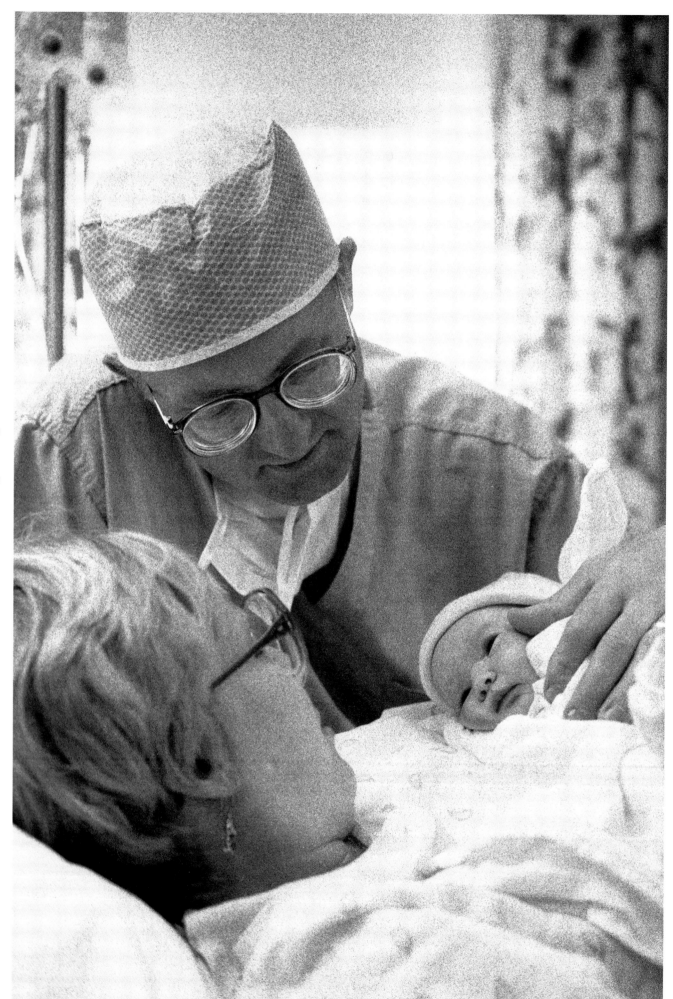

6:15 a.m., Monday
*Emma Preusse Mitchell was born at 5:59 a.m., and by shortly after 6:00 a.m., Mark and Julia were alone and quietly admiring their beautiful girl.*

Jane Gleeson

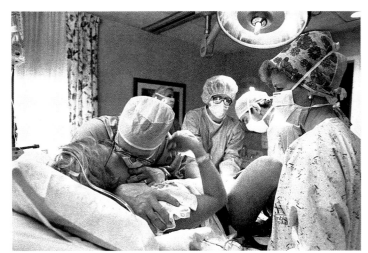

6:00 a.m., Monday
*Dr. Mark Mitchell, a
Milwaukee pediatri-
cian, kisses his wife,
Julia, a nurse, in
sweet emotion at the
birth of their daugh-
ter. "You did just
great — I couldn't
have done it!" They
are in the birthing
room of Columbia
Hospital, Milwaukee.*

Jane Gleeson

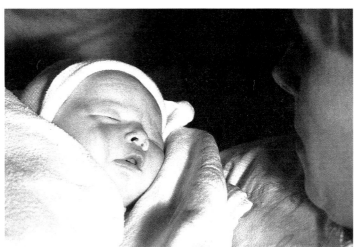

6:30 a.m., Monday
*Tender moments of
reacquaintance for
Julia and Emma.*

Jane Gleeson

6:52 p.m., Sunday
*Debra Braatz was walking her brittany spaniel, Sadie, at Aztalan State Park, Aztalan. She has lived in Wisconsin all of her life and now works as a physical education instructor at the local elementary school.*

T. J. Florian

10:30 p.m., Saturday
*Ball practice at
Southview Park in
Neenah. The team is
sponsored by the
Neenah Fire Depart-
ment and had not yet
played a game.*

Bonnie Auxier

11:45 a.m., Monday
*Ground crew prepares the infield for the Brewers vs. Detroit game.*

Gary Dineen

10:00 a.m., Monday
*Amish buggy traveling on Military Road at the Greenlake/Columbia County border.*

James R. Koepnick

10:00 a.m., Friday
*Leroy Ciscon, town of Worcester, cuts grass on Joe Carek's farmstead.*

Erol Reyal

**THE BIG CLICK:** *Photographing Wisconsin*

Project Coordinator
   Jane Collins


Assistant Coordinator
   Erol Reyal


Project Committee
   James Enright
   Al Barber
   Kathy Bump


Editors
   Chip Henderson
   Jane Collins
   Nichole Parisoe
   Betsy Jones
   Marie Wright


A special documentary has been prepared by The Big Click: Photographing Wisconsin television network and is edited by Ruth Ravve. Stations: WISN-TV, WMTV, WLUK-TV, WSAW-TV, WEAU-TV.

Our thanks to Milwaukee Institute of Art & Design for offices and staff.

## HOTEL CONTRIBUTORS

The American Club
Highland Drive
Kohler, WI 53044
414-457-8000

Best Western
Fountain Park Motor Inn
930 N. 8th Street
Sheboygan, WI 53081
414-458-4641

Best Western
Midway Motor Lodge of Green Bay
780 Packer Drive
Green Bay, WI 54304
414-499-3161

East Highland Bed & Breakfast
Rt. 1, Box 484
Phillips, WI 54555
715-339-3492

Flambeau Forest Resort
HCR 67, Box 65
Winter, WI 54896
715-332-5236

Hospitality Inn
4400 S. 27th Street
Milwaukee, WI 53221
414-282-8800

Howard Johnson Lodge
2001 N. Mountain Road
Wausau, WI 54401
715-842-0711

Kewaunee KOA
P.O. Box 5
Terraqua Drive
Kewaunee, WI 54216
414-388-4007

Pride's English Manor
Bed & Breakfast
204 S. 2nd Street
Tomahawk, WI 54487
715-453-7670

Village Inn Motel
1060 W. Fulton Street
Waupaca, WI 54981
800-626-6391

Wagon Trail Resort
1041 Highway 22
Ellison Bay, WI 54210
414-854-2385

West Harbor Resort
Rt. 1, Box 222
Washington Island, WI 54246
414-847-2225

## CONTRIBUTORS

TMS Incorporated
Racine

Modus Operandi: Graphics Inc.
Milwaukee

Franklin Press Inc.
Milwaukee

Betty's Chocolate Nook Ltd.
Greenfield

Custom Screen Limited
Milwaukee

Brookfield Hills
Brookfield

Minuteman Press
Milwaukee

Elm Grove Massage Therapy
Elm Grove

Paul Smith: Design
Milwaukee

Hunter Zigman Inc.
Milwaukee

Pak Mail
Waukesha

Helix Photoart Rental
Milwaukee

Mary Ann Picard
Wauwatosa

Mike Brawn
Milwaukee

Earl R. Davison
Milwaukee

Cyd Sowlles
New Berlin

Aerial Work Platforms Inc.
Waukesha

Eagle Video Service
Phillips

Von Stiehl Winery
Algoma

W. P. Gumm
Anvil Lake

Harmann Photo
Algoma

Wisconsin Veterans Home
King

R & R Sport Fishing Charters
Kewaunee

Shoreline Resort Charters
Gills Rock

Washington Island Ferry Line
Washington Island

Grand Seasons Hotel
Waupaca

Information Technology
UW-Stevens Point

Jim's Union 76 Station
Waupaca

## PHOTOGRAPHERS

Timothy G. Abler
Milwaukee

Robert J. Alberte, Jr.
Milwaukee

Ralph E. Adamson
Plymouth

Melody Ankrum
Oshkosh

Sam Arendt
Plymouth

Lila Aryan
Whitefish Bay

Bonnie L. Auxier
Neenah

Al Balinsky
Milwaukee

Al Barber
Milwaukee

Debra J. Bartlein
Milwaukee

Darryl R. Beers
Green Bay

Michael J. Bersch
Bayside

Sue Boyer
Oconomowoc

Mike Brisson
Stevens Point

Bruce W. Buchanan
Milwaukee

Kathy Bump
Milwaukee

Paul C. Butterbrodt
Milwaukee

Mary Catanese-Pugens
Milwaukee

Shelly Anne Cavins
Appleton

David (Chip) Chapiewsky
Madison

Gary G. Dineen
Cedarburg

Peter S. Draves
Milwaukee

James Enright
Racine

T. J. Florian
Waukesha

Jenny Frankovis
Milwaukee

Mary Freeman
Fond du Lac

Jane Gleeson
Milwaukee

Mark Gubin
Milwaukee

Duane W. Hopp
Mt. Horeb

John Iwatta
Oshkosh

Barbara L. Jakopac
Milwaukee

Thomas M. Jernigan
Milwaukee

Mary Jones
Oshkosh

Meg Jones
Wausau

Darryl Jordan
Milwaukee

James R. Koepnick
Oshkosh

Bruce Krueger
Milwaukee

James R. Labre
Neenah

Mary Langenfeld
Madison

Jon Lee
Coon Valley

Fred Jay Loomis
Kenosha

Marny A. Malin
Greenfield

Charles (Chip) Manthey
Green Bay

Sarah McEneany
Shorewood

Robert Melkonian
Milwaukee

Thomas Moran
Greendale

Scott Morris
Milwaukee

Scott Neuville
Chicago, IL

Shawn J. O'Malley
Gurnee, IL

Thomas J. Parker
Iron Mountain

Nancy Pass
Milwaukee

Jeff Peters
Ashland

Guy Peterson
West Bend

Mark S. Picard
Wauwatosa

Todd Ponath
West Bend

Erol Reyal
Milwaukee

Craig Robinson
Minneapolis, MN

Scott A. Schutz
Kenosha

Scott Smetana
Milwaukee

Timothy P. Snopek
Waukesha

Henry H. Smith
West Allis

Minimay Smith
Winnebago

Robert L. Smith
Shorewood

Richard L. Staszewski
La Crosse

Michael R. Steineke
Oshkosh

G. Glen Walton
La Crescent, MN

Dr. Leroy L. Zacher
Oshkosh